Memories on Muslin:

1934 Athelstan Quilt Blocks & Depression-era Quilting

Memories on Muslin:

1934 Athelstan Quilt Blocks & Depression-era Quilting

www.trishafaye.com

Copyright ©2018 by Trisha Faye

ISBN-13: 978-1534848641

ISBN-10: 1534848649

This book is dedicated to Nellie & Doris Morris.

I doubt Nellie Morris knew that by collecting these appliquéd quilt blocks in 1934 they would remain as a lasting tribute to the family and friendships of Athelstan, Iowa eighty years later. The squares remained together all these years, stitched calico pieces that are reminders of the connections once held. It's time to tell their story.

In honor and tribute to:

Doris & Mother (Nellie and Doris Morris), Betty Balch, John Balch, Beverly Ruth Barnett, Dorothy Barnett, Darlene Booher, Leona Booher, Charls Bownes, Evelyn Bownes, Maxine Bownes, Minnie & Josie Bownes, Mrs. E.J. Bownes, Leona Mae Byrns, Jean Marie Carroll, Lelah Clark, Kate Fidler, Katie Kemery, Norma Gean Kemery, Rex Morris, Grace Murray, Georgia Older, Deliliah Rusco, Berneice Scott, Thelma Weaver, Dean Weese, and three unnamed people, anonymous to us forever.

With Special Thanks:

Special thanks to these women for their part in telling the stories of these squares and helping to bring them to their new home at the Taylor County Historical Museum:

Rosalyn Cummings (descendant of Evelyn Bownes), current Director of the Taylor County Historical Museum

Leona Mae (Byrns) Stephenson (the youngest person represented on a block)

Bonnie Polston (descendant of Maxine Bownes)

Helen Jansen, past Director of the Taylor County Historical Museum.

Thanks also goes to Sandi Salen and the wonderful volunteers at the Taylor County Historical Museum for their dedication and warm welcome. Everyone's help was invaluable and much appreciated.

Meeting these women, the other descendants of these Athelstan people from the past, and the Bedford community has been a high point in my life. Sharing the excitement of finding the common links of these squares is only surpassed by the pleasure of meeting the many people I've come to admire.

Thank you also to Brenda Weed, proprietor of The Farmer's Dotter, the quilter's retreat where I stayed when I was in Iowa. I thought I'd died and gone to heaven amidst all the quilts and the décor of vintage pieces.

Memories are like a patchwork quilt....each section is sewn together, to be wrapped around us for comfort and warmth |in the years to come.
~Author Unknown

This set of thirty 1934 quilt squares now happily reside at their new home. Stop by to take a peek and see some of the other great displays. This wonderful museum is truly an Iowa treasure.

Taylor County Historical Museum
1001 Pollock Blvd.
Bedford, IA 50833

Tuesday – Sunday: 1 pm to 4 pm
Monday: Chance or appointment

Phone: (712) 523-2041

Website:
http://taylorcomuseum.wixsite.com/taylorco

Open from April through December

Table of Contents

Prices
Bonnie & Clyde
Dust Bowl
Fireside Chats
Milestones 1932-1934

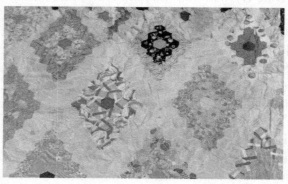

This is one of the three quilt tops that were with the set of 1934 quilt squares. It's 'The Diamond Field' pattern, a variation of the quilt known as 'French Bouquet', 'Bouquet', 'Rose Garden', or 'Grandmother's Flower Garden'. The pattern for The Diamond Field ran in *The Kansas City Star* on April 13, 1932, and in the *Lansing State Journal* in Michigan in 1933. Other newspapers probably printed it also.

Introduction

'One man's trash is another man's treasure.'

I don't know who to attribute this quote to, yet it's the perfect quote to begin the story of the 1934 Athelstan Iowa Quilt Blocks. That's how I acquired this set of thirty quilt blocks that are truly a treasure.

I did not know that stopping at a yard sale one afternoon would alter my life several years later. It was a typical, sunny Southern California day (around 2005 or 2006). It was a Friday and I'd driven out to a friend's condo in Palm Springs for a few hours. While leaving town to return home, I saw a sign staked at the edge of the street. Giant black letters proclaimed 'YARD SALE' with an arrow pointing left.

I wondered if yard sales in Palm Springs were any different than the ones at home. I quickly turned down the side street and stopped to browse the graveled front yard, littered with tables and 'good deals' covering most of the yard area. I walked around quickly without spending much time. Videos for $2 each, stacks of paperback books, tires, the usual miscellaneous assortment of unwanted items. I didn't see anything that called my name.

Then ... I spotted the table with bedding, towels and such. I honestly don't remember what else was there because a laundry basket with quilted fabrics caught my attention right away. I looked closer and it appeared to be several quilt tops in the basket, pieced but never completed into quilts. There were some quilt squares nestled in amongst the quilt tops, some Sunbonnet Sues and Overall Bills. They appeared to be older fabrics. There wasn't a price on the basket or on the individual pieces.

Another quilt top that was purchased with the set of 1934 quilt squares.

Over the prior years, I'd acquired a few old quilts at antique stores. A very few, because I usually couldn't afford them, they were typically priced way out of my budget. Hoping that I could afford to purchase at least one of the quilt tops, or even just one of the squares, I approached the lady that appeared to be in charge of the yard sale.

I tried very hard to appear nonchalant and almost bored. "How much do you want for the quilt tops?" I asked, knowing I had $20 in my wallet and could run to an ATM to get another $20. Higher than that, I'd be out of luck.

"Well, they're pretty old," she answered. (Duh! I thought to myself. Why do you think I want one so much? But I wisely kept my thoughts to myself.) I forget now if her answer was fifteen or twenty dollars. All I remember is being so excited because I had enough money in my wallet.

"For each one?" I asked, trying to quickly decide which one I wanted most.

"For all of them."

Poker face intact, I calmly said, "I'll take them." Inside I was jumping up and down, almost doing cartwheels as I strolled to the car (trying very hard not to run) to get the cash for my new treasures. Handing her the money, I started to take them all out of the laundry basket and she said, "Take the basket too."

I think I said thank you. I'm sure I did, but I was almost delirious and trying so hard not to show my delight so she wouldn't snatch the basket back and raise the price. I sat the basket in the back seat and drove away as fast as I could without attracting the attention of any Palm Springs police officers.

Arriving home an hour and a half later, I proudly carried my yard sales treasures inside. Lifting each piece out, one at a time, revealed that I now had three pieced and unquilted quilt tops, along with a set of thirty Sunbonnet Sue and Overall Bill quilt squares.

Each of the squares had a name stitched on it, except for three. The piece de resistance was one square that was stitched with 'To Doris, From Mother, 1934'. I was ecstatic!

Any of the quilt tops, by itself, was worth far more than what I paid for the entire lot. Two were machine stitched and were simply pieced blocks in no particular pattern. One top, my favorite of the three, was completely hand stitched. It consists of little tiny hexagons making up a pattern similar to 'Grandmothers Flower Garden', except the usual circle of hexagons had one additional hexagon on each side, creating a diamond type design. I'd never seen one in this pattern before.

The wheels in my brain started turning. If the quilt squares had names on them and the year 1934 on one of the squares…then somewhere, someplace in 1934, all of these names were connected in some way. Maybe they all weren't connected to each other, but they must have had a common link to Doris and Mother.

Making a list of all of the names on the squares, I added notes for each. Which ones had matching fabrics, same surnames, similar stitching? On many, I made the note 'very young or very old', due to the quality of the stitching. I sat down at the computer several times, putting various combinations of names in the search engine, trying to discover a common denominator among some of the names.

I didn't find any answers. Their secret was to remain hidden for several more years.

I moved from California. The squares, along with the quilt tops and my other antique quilts were packed up for the move. They stayed packed away for three years, while I moved to Arizona for a year and then on to Texas.

About two years after moving to Texas, I was going through things in my closet one day. You know how things tend to accumulate when your back is turned and pretty soon you have little piles all over? Oh, not yours? Well, at least in my closet that happens. I think it's like the little dust bunnies that procreate while you're busy with life. You turn around and...pouf...there they are!

I was busy that day, probably around June or July 2010. I hauled things out of the closet, going through clothes, filling a bag for the thrift store and throwing things in the trash. I sorted presents purchased ahead of time from extra toiletries and lotions. I rummaged through boxes I'd brought to Texas but hadn't gone through recently.

I opened one box and started sorting, all the little miscellaneous things that tend to accumulate without much thought. I pulled out a yellow legal sheet, folded in quarters, with names and notes written on it. I was surprised to see the list of names from the quilt squares, that I'd written in California. I hadn't been successful in my search before. But, who knows, maybe now?

Sitting down at the computer that evening, I started searching for names, not really expecting to find anything again. I ran down the list, adding two or three at a time. A website popped in the search results that appeared to have several names!

The 1925 census from Athelstan, Iowa appeared. Scrolling through this list I found six names that matched squares in my set. Woohoo! I was doing the happy dance. I'd discovered a link. I felt that if six of thirty names were in one place, this town of Athelstan, Iowa, wherever it was, had to be the common link.

Actually, six names of twenty-seven matched, not six of thirty, since three squares were unsigned. Three of the squares were completed with solid colors of red, black, and blue, typically associated with Amish dolls and quilts. They also did not have any names added, typical also of Amish beliefs to not make graven images of themselves. Although there weren't names on these three squares, I knew that there are also many Amish in Iowa, which gave weight to the Athelstan, Iowa connection.

After all the unsuccessful attempts before, in less than an hour I'd discovered an Athelstan connection for six names. The 1925 Athelstan Iowa census listed:

Darlene Booher, 1-year-old

Leona Booher, 2 years old

Katie Fidler, 38 years old

Georgia Older, 39 years old

Delilah Rusco, 2 years old

Berneice Scott, 1-year-old

Ah ha! Add nine years to get to 1934 and these girls would be ten to eleven years old, possibly nine to twelve years old, depending on when the census was taken and when their birthdays were.

That explains my notes from several years earlier: 'very young or very old'.

I found a listing for the Athelstan Cemetery which listed Georgia Older again and also E.J. Bownes, another name on my list of quilt squares. My notes on Mrs. E.J. Bownes and Georgia Older said 'same stitching and same fabrics'. Further research proved that Eliza Jane Bownes was Georgia Older's mother. Eliza Jane (May 4, 1858-May 15, 1938) was seventy-six when the squares were completed and most likely Georgia made the square for herself and her mother. Since both squares have possibly some of the neatest stitching out of all the squares, I tend to lean towards Georgia making both squares, thinking that Eliza's eyesight may have diminished in her later years. But, maybe not. Maybe Eliza's eyesight was fine and her hand was steady, and she made both squares. I can document Georgia and Eliza were mother and daughter, both living in Athelstan, Iowa, and both are buried in Athelstan Cemetery. I can't document which one of the two made the squares. That part shall forever remain a mystery.

Athelstan Cemetery holds the remains of many family members connected to the quilt squares: Balch, Booher, Byrns, Fidler, Kemery, Morris, Older, Rusco, Scott, Weaver and Weese. According to a cemetery list by Iowa Gravestone, at least six of the people commemorated by squares in this set are buried there: Leona Booher, Mrs. E.J. (Eliza Jane) Bownes, Evelyn Bownes, Maxine Bownes, Georgia Older and Berneice Scott.

Also laid to rest in this small tightly knit community are others that stitched squares. Eva Marie Byrns created the square for her daughter, Leona, who was only 18-months old at the time. Zelma Weese made a square for her son, Dean, who was two years old. China Scott may have been the one to make squares for her daughter Berneice Scott and possibly for Thelma Weaver, her step-granddaughter.

Doris' parents, Nellie and Charles Morris, are buried at Athelstan Cemetery, along with one brother, Gerald, and her sister, Vivian Parker. Many other families members of the women and children memorialized on these squares are buried here, just outside of the old town.

8

Thank goodness for the internet. Before I've bemoaned how there is so much information available for public access, but now it was working in my favor.

The "hunt" was on!

Over the next few years, I discovered information about more of the people that stitched these quilt blocks so many years ago. There's still more to discover. But in this journey, my greatest joy has been making the connections with the Iowa women connected to these squares from the past.

The Stitch and Chatter Club

The discovery of these quilt squares in a yard sale brought more than pieces of muslin to our attention. They brought several mysteries with them.

From the stitching on one square 'From Mother To Doris', it appeared that this set of squares was a gift. Birthday or Christmas present? Thankfully Eva Byrns put Leona's age (18 months) on her daughter's square. Upon finding out that Leona's birthday was in June, it was apparent that this was a Christmas present.

But, why did Nellie Morris decide on this gift? Did she see the idea for a friendship quilt and want to make one for Doris? Did she simply start asking her friends and neighbors, and Doris' friends to stitch up a square for Doris?

In an email conversation with Leona, she mentioned that she remembered her mother being in an Athelstan quilt guild.

But that's as much as we knew – at that time.

When I took the squares to Iowa, to present them to the museum at a Quilt Tea in August 2014, Helen Janson and her daughter, Jeanne shared their own discovery with us. They'd been busy researching and they found some new information that shed some light on how the squares most likely began. There was a quilting club in Athelstan, and it formed in late 1934.

Jeanne and Helen shared five newspaper snippets from *The Bedford Times-Press* that mentioned the newly formed Stitch and Chatter Club.

September 6, 1934:

FORM NEW CLUB:

Elect Officers – Harriett Frazier is President

A group of Athelstan ladies have formed a new club, which will be known as "The Stitch and Chatter Club". The following officers were elected: President, Harriet Frazier; vice president, Alma Lyons; secretary, Katie Kemery; treasurer, Katie Fidler. Mrs. Frazier was hostess to the club today, Sept. 6.

...The ladies of Athelstan and vicinity finished the second of two quilts Friday they had pieced and quilted for the F.S. Fidler family who lost their household goods by fire recently.

October 18, 1934:

Club Knots Comforts

The Stitch and Chatter club met Thursday at the home of Mrs. Ida Bownes. The afternoon was spent in knotting comforts. Mrs. Marjorie Book became a new member of the club. Mrs. Hilda Rusco will be hostess at the next meeting.

November 15, 1934:

Club Has Quilting

The Stitch and Chatter club met with Mrs. Jennie Rusco Thursday. The day was spent in quilting. Guests were Ruby Jenkins, who became a new member of the club, Mrs. O.P. Pettigrew and Ethel Sickles. The next meeting will be with Mrs. Ida King.

Donate To Church

The ladies of the Stitch and Chatter club served lunch and dinner election day, clearing twenty dollars, which will be applied to the fund to repair the Athelstan Baptist church.

November 29, 1934:

Ladies Clean Church

The ladies of the Stitch and Chatter club, who had the Athelstan Baptist church repaired recently, met Tuesday afternoon and again Friday and cleaned the church.

Club Has Quilting

The Stitch and Chatter club met at the home of Violet Woods, Thursday. Fourteen members were present. The afternoon was spent in quilting. An all day meeting will be held at the home of Bess Rusco, Friday, Nov. 30.

December 13, 1934:

Mrs. Rusco Entertains

The Stitch and Chatter club met at the home of Bess Rusco, Thursday, Dec. 6. The day was spent in quilting. Verne Books and Mrs. J.D. Brown were guests. Mrs. Ruby Treece will be the next hostess.

Maybe some things don't change as much through the years as we think. Days spent quilting together and socializing, making warm quilts for a family in the community in need, raising funds to repair a local church, spending time cleaning the church; all activities that women and their quilt club did then – and do now.

The 1934
Athelstan Quilt Squares

From Mother, To Doris, 1934

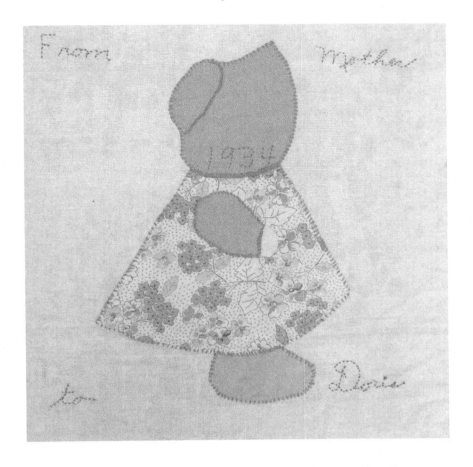

Our lives are like quilts...bit and pieces, joy, and sorrow stitched with love.

~Author Unknown

Betty Balch

A quilt will warm your body and comfort your soul.
~Author Unknown

John Balch

**Our lives are like quilts - bits and pieces,
joy and sorrow, stitched with love.**
~Author Unknown

Beverly Ruth Barnett

**Really I don't dislike to cook,
but what you cook is eaten so quickly.
When you sew, you have something that will last to
show for your efforts.**
~Elizabeth Travis Johnson

Dorothy Barnett

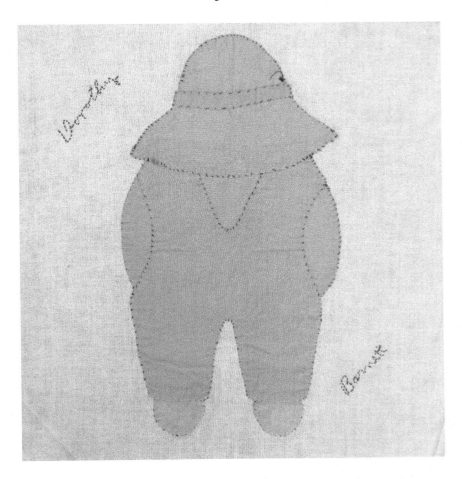

All my scattering moments are taken up with my needle.

~ Ellen Birdseye Wheaton, 1851

Darlene Booher

When life throws you scraps, make a quilt.
~Author Unknown

Leona Booher

**Chains do not hold a marriage together.
It is threads, hundreds of tiny threads which
sew people together through the years.**
~Simone Signoret

Charls Bownes

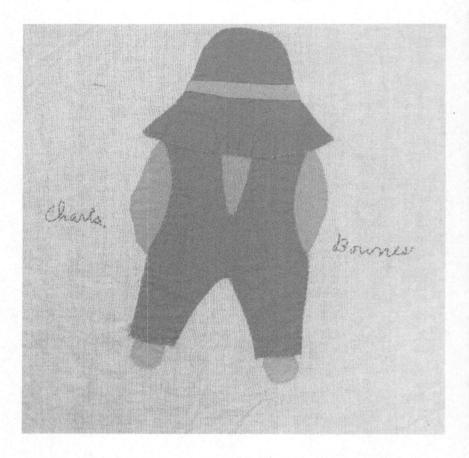

Good friends are like quilts – they age with you yet never lose their warmth.

Author Unknown

Evelyn Bownes

Useful and ornamental needlework, knitting, and netting are capable of being made, not only sources of personal gratification, but of high moral benefit, and the means of developing in surpassing loveliness and grace, some of the highest and noblest feelings of the soul.

~Author unknown, from The Ladies' Work Table Book, 1845

Maxine Bownes

Memories are stitched with love.
~Author Unknown

Minnie & Josie Bownes

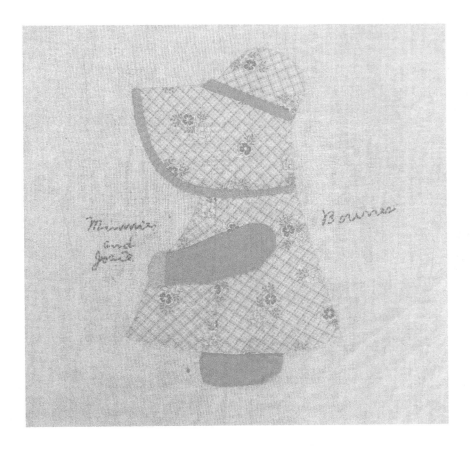

In the crazy quilt of life, I'm glad you're in my block of friends.

~Author Unknown

Mrs. E. J. Bownes

A family is a patchwork of love.
~Author Unknown

Leona Mae Byrns

Those who sleep under a quilt, sleep under a blanket of love.
~Author Unknown

Jean Marie Carroll

She watched and taught the girls that sang at their embroidery frames while the great silk flowers grew from their needles.

~Louise Jordan Miln, The Feast of Lanterns

Lelah Clark

**From the manner in which a woman draws
her thread at every stitch of her needlework,
any other woman can surmise her thoughts.**
~Honore de Balzac

Katie Fidler

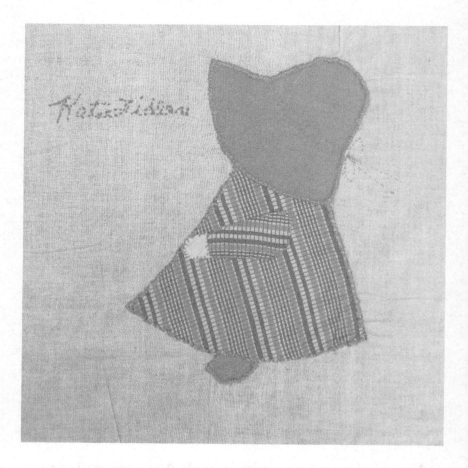

Quilters know all the angles.
~Author Unknown

Katie Kemery

A bed without a quilt is like a sky without stars.
~Author Unknown

Norma Gean Kemery

Good friends are like Quilts.
They age with you, yet never lose their
warmth.
~Author Unknown

Rex Morris

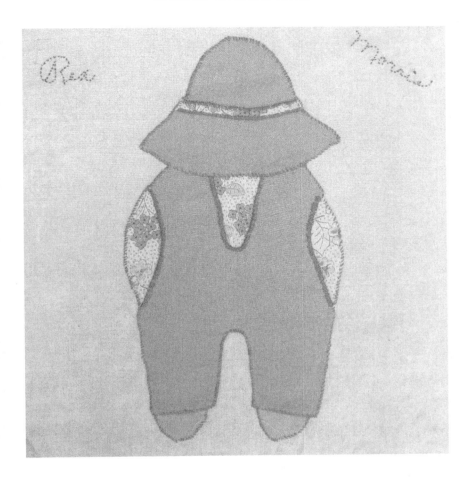

Old quilters never die, they just fray away.
Old quilters never die, they just go batts.
Old quilters never die, they just go to pieces.
~Author Unknown

Grace Murray

Quilting is like love...do it with abandon.
~Author Unknown

Georgia Older

Grandma quilts have love in every stitch.
~Author Unknown

Deliliah Rusco

To quilt or not to quilt?
What a silly question!
~Author Unknown

Berneice Scott

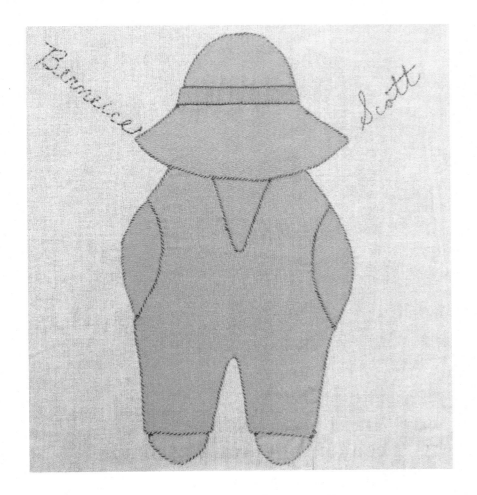

**Blessed are the piece makers.
Blessed are the children of piece makers... for
they shall inherit the quilts.**
~Author Unknown

Thelma Weaver

I cannot count my day complete
'Til needle, thread and fabric meet.
~Author Unknown

Dean Weese

Take your needle, my child, and work at your pattern; it will come out a rose by and by. Life is like that; one stitch at a time taken patiently, and the pattern will come out all right, like embroidery.
- Oliver Wendell Holmes

Dean Weese

(Second Square)

**Quilters never grow old,
they just go to pieces.**
~Author Unknown

Unnamed Square 1

Stitch your stress away.
~Author Unknown

Unnamed Square 2

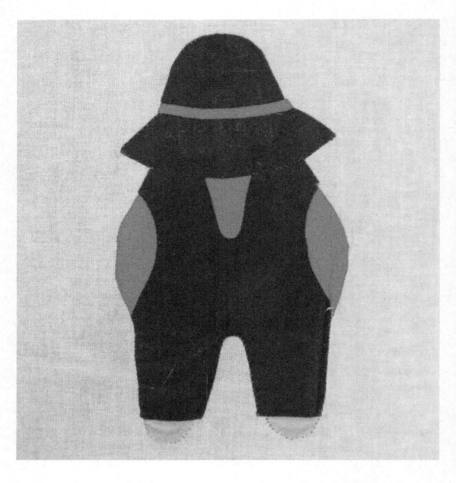

Any day spent sewing, is a good day.
~Author Unknown

Unnamed Square 3

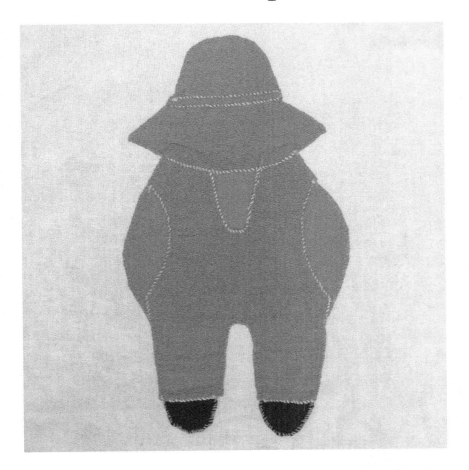

Memories are stitched with love.
~Author Unknown

The People Behind the Squares

Initially, I wanted to share everything that I'd discovered in my quest to get to know my adopted Athelstan 'family'. However, in the interest of preserving the privacy of the descendants still living, I won't share all that I've found.

I feel compelled to share the story of these quilt squares. I believe they crossed my path and were entrusted to me until I handed them over to the historical museum. My mission, as I chose to accept it, (spoken in a far from accurate James Bond dialect)...is to honor the women of the past, the creators of these small muslin slices of history.

These blocks never made it into a finished quilt. Yet, Doris treasured the blocks and kept them all together for all of her life. Children and grandchildren were born. The squares remained together, probably sitting on a shelf or tucked away in a drawer or trunk. And still, she kept them, these memories of her childhood. Memories of friends and neighbors lived on even as they were tucked away until the end of Doris' earthly life found her processions sold and scattered.

Tracing the lineage of the squares has not been easy. Athelstan was a fairly small rural town. Families were connected in many tenuous ways. Trying to get a clear look at who was related to who is like tracing an interconnected Celtic knot.

Olders' were related to Kemery's and Bownes, Hayes, and Balchs'. Sickels' were related to Rusco's and Older's and later on Bownes. Booher's were related to Hayes and Balch's and Older's. Whew! It makes my head spin just trying to figure out the genealogy lines of these thirty squares.

GEORGIA OLDER & MRS. E.J. BOWNES

Two of my favorite blocks are from Georgia Older and Mrs. E. J. Bownes. Not only is the stitching beautifully done, I love the story behind the squares.

Georgia's square of a Sunbonnet Sue in her neatly stitched bonnet matches the fabrics and stitching of Mrs. E.J. Bownes's Overall Bill. Georgia was forty-nine years old at the time the squares were created. Her mother, Eliza Jane (Hayes) Bownes was seventy-six. Most likely, Georgia stitched both blocks, although we'll never know for sure. Eliza Jane lived for four more years after these squares were created, passing away May 16, 1938.

Georgia married Melvin Older on September 24, 1902. Melvin was postmaster of Athelstan for thirty years. Georgia served as assistant postmistress, city treasurer and secretary of the school board. They had one daughter, Opha, who had been married for ten years when the quilt squares were made.

48

Through the Bownes family line, Georgia was related to the many Bownes' children that made squares for this friendship quilt.

Two sisters, Evelyn Bownes and Maxine Bownes, made squares for Doris' quilt. Their father, Fred Bownes, was Georgia Older's brother. Maxine (Georgia Maxine, named after her Aunt Georgia) was a little older than some of the girls, at nineteen years old. In 1938, she married Donald Carroll, half-brother to Jean Marie Carroll, another creator of a quilt square.

Evelyn, a little younger and only nine years old when she made her square, ended up marrying another local boy, Lyle Sickels. The Sickels, Ruscos, and Olders were related also. Evelyn's daughter, Rosalyn, shared a story with me. In an email, she told how they went to visit Great Aunt Georgia one time when she was young. She was impressed with how wealthy Great Aunt Georgia and Uncle Melvin were because their outhouse was wallpapered! Now, I've visited many an outhouse myself, having relatives in Missouri - and even having one ourselves in Arkansas when I was a teenager - but I've never seen a wallpapered outhouse.

BALCH and BOOHER

The Balch's and Booher's are also related. Viola Jane (Paris) Booher, grandmother to sisters Leona and Darlene Booher, is the daughter of Isabella (Kauble) Paris', from Isabella's first marriage.

After Isabella's husband died, she married Andrew Hayes and had two more children, Grace (Hayes) Balch and Joseph Hayes. Grace Balch had two children, Betty and John, who each have a quilt square.

If my tracing the family trees is correct, Leona & Darlene Booher's grandmother (Viola Jane) is the half-sister to Betty & John Balch's mother (Grace Balch).

Betty and John are possibly related to Georgia Older. Their grandfather is Andrew Jackson Hayes, and Georgia's mother is Eliza (Hayes) Bownes. There's got to be a family connection between Andrew Hayes and Eliza Hayes, but I haven't been able to find the link yet. On a side note, in 1868 a brother of Andrew J. Hayes also married a Booher (Martha). Lots of sisters married brothers, and sisters married cousins, etc., causing lots of confusion a hundred years later as we try to trace these not-documented-so-well family lines.

LEONA MAE BYRNS

The youngest person with a quilt square here, the only one with an age embroidered on her square, is Leona Mae Byrns. Leona's mother, Eva Marie (Black) Byrns, embellished the green bonnet with decorative stitches, and then added her age at the bottom of the square 'Age 18 mos'.

Leona is now a great-grandmother and is still in the local area. In an email, Leona shared that she remembers her mother attending the Athelstan Quilt Guild.

At the Quilt Tea at the museum where I presented the squares to the museum in 2014, Jeanne and Helen Janson brought copies of the *Bedford Times-Press*. In September 1934, a new club was formed in Athelstan – The Stitch and Chatter Club.

At the tea, another Athelstan descendant brought some similar squares with different names embroidered on the blocks. One other descendant mentioned having a quilt out of the blocks. Evidently, many of the women in this new quilting club exchanged blocks with each other.

Leona helped clear up one mystery of the squares. I was assuming that the quilt squares were a gift for Doris because of how her square was embroidered 'From Mother, To Doris'. But I wasn't sure if it was a birthday or Christmas gift.

With Leona's age of 18-months as a clue, I asked Leona when her birthday was. She replied it was June 7, 1933. With that birthdate, she would have been 18 months old in December of 1934. That answered one of my many questions. The quilt squares must have been a Christmas gift for Doris.

DEAN WEESE

Besides Doris' friends that contributed squares for this set of friendship blocks, Doris's mother's friends in The Stitch and Chatter Club also contributed quilt blocks.

Another toddler besides Leona Mae is represented by a quilt block, Dean Weese. Dean Weese has *two* quilt blocks here, one a Sunbonnet Sue and one an Overall Bill. Why two? I don't know. I'll probably never know the answer to this little mystery.

Dean was two years old at the time, so it wasn't that his mother was expecting and didn't know whether she was having a boy or a girl. Did she like both patterns and didn't know which one she wanted to use? Did they need another block to even out the set at thirty? I do know that Dean (b. 9/27/1932, d. 6/23/2011) didn't sew his own block, so his mother most likely did.

Zelma's obituary states:

"Zelma Leona Smith Weese, daughter of Frank and Effie Dye Smith, was born on February 18, 1914 on a farm north of Athelstan, Iowa. She departed this life on August 28, 1996 at Heartland East Hospital in St. Joseph, Missouri at the age of 82 years, six months and ten days.

Zelma grew to adulthood in Athelstan, where she attended the Athelstan School and the Holiness Church. On January 1, 1931, she was united in marriage at the home of her parents to William B.

52

[enjamin] Weese of Sheridan, Missouri. To this union four sons were born, Dean Laverne, Dwayne Leroy, Clarence Melvin and Gary Eldon.

Zelma spent her life as a wife, mother and homemaker. While raising a family of her own, when sickness or emergencies arose, she was always ready and willing to help care for her many nieces and nephews, who loved and respected her. She enjoyed gardening, canning and all other aspects of farm life. Her favorite hobby was making quilts for her children and grandchildren."

Quilting -- it never does leave your blood, does it?

BERNEICE SCOTT AND THELMA WEAVER

These square have two completely different last names, yet the fabrics match and the stitching is the same. There had to be a connection between the two.

Research shows that they are.

Who stitched the squares? That question I can't answer; the stitching will remain another mystery. It could have been China Scott, Joyce Scott, Thelma Weaver, or Berneice Scott. My best guess is that China Scott stitched the squares for her young daughter and her older daughter's step-daughter.

The 1925 census shows that James & China Scott had five children in the house, Berneice was one year old and Joyce was eight years old.

Fast forward to 1931. Neighbor Raymond Weaver's wife, Fern Gollady, dies leaving him with three children: Marie, Duane, and Thelma. (ages still unknown to me).

A few years later, in 1933, Raymond married Joyce Scott, Berneice's older sister. Joyce may have sewn the two squares. But I think as a young wife and new step-mother to three children, she probably had her hands full.

Berneice may have sewn them, but the stitching (to me) looks more controlled and even than a ten-year-old could execute, although I may be wrong. Not knowing Thelma's age, she may or may not have stitched the two squares. However, my best guess is China Scott made them.

Who needs to read mysteries when there are real-life mysteries to solve?

Just a note here, if you've counted names or squares here, you'll see only twenty-nine quilt blocks. Yet, I've mentioned a set of thirty squares. There is one additional square in the set. The person represented on that square is still living and doesn't wish to be mentioned, so I've honored her wish and not included her block or name here. So, no, it wasn't an error or faulty counting. Consider the missing 30th square to be just one more mystery to go along with the others.

Early Athelstan

Athelstan, Iowa joined the long list of small rural towns declining into oblivion. Thanks to Doris's mother, Nellie, local town women and Doris' friends, they left a memory of their friendships and connections, stitched in calico. Doris may have never pieced the thirty squares together into a quilt, but she treasured them enough to keep them together for the rest of her life. Athelstan may no longer be a town, but these calico connections remain, a cotton and muslin monument to lives touching each other.

Sitting on the Iowa/Missouri border, Athelstan lies west of the Platte River, a tributary of the Missouri River. Fish in the Platte River include Alligator Gar, Channel Catfish, Flathead Catfish, Freshwater Drum and Small Mouth Buffalo. Fishing in rural areas such as this, especially during the 1930's was enjoyment for many, but more importantly, a food source for feeding families in the economic aftermath of the depression. Betty Balch, eleven years old when she made her quilt square (and probably her brother John's square also), met her future husband Cleo Ott Houchin while fishing on the Platte River by Athelstan.

This small town also has a split personality. Straddling the Iowa/Missouri border, Athelstan at one point lay claim to both states.

A previously undated article, reprinted in the *Bedford Times Press* on 11/7/1974, highlights Athelstan history. I saw a clue in the article "William Large, settled on a 640-acre farm a mile west of Athelstan in 1864, lived there until his death as did his son, J. W., 'who died in February of this year.' The only problem I saw was that John W. Large, son of William & Lavina Hankins Large, died in Athelstan on December 29, 1940, not in February. Well, December is close to February. Its close enough that I tend to believe the article was written sometime in 1941. It also tells a little of the stories that are passed on that we tend to take for gospel truth. February …. December … only 60 days apart, not horribly important. It goes to show that our memories are not perfect and perhaps anything that gets 'passed down' may have some inconsistencies and errors. So a great deal of this history gleaned from small facts here and there, may need to be taken with the proverbial grain of salt.

Two early settlers are mentioned in the article, although there were probably more in the early settlement. Louis Tackett (Lewis Tackkett on the cemetery list) had a 40-acre farm in the west of what was then Athelstan. Samuel Woods had 200 acres in what is at that time, Athelstan.

 Both Louis/Lewis (died in 1901 at 79 years old) and his daughter Nancy Tackett Swett (died in 1933, approximately 70 years old) are buried in Athelstan Cemetery. Samuel Woods (died 9/8/1878), his first wife Mary (died 4/3/1864) and at least several of his children from his second wife, Nancy, (James and John) are all buried at Athelstan Cemetery.

The original article states, "Late in 1887 the Chicago Great-Western Railway was built through

Athelstan and the Woods and Tackett farms were sub-divided to form the town of Iona, Mo."

Miles Martin was the first postmaster. "The post office was later moved into Iowa at which time the name of the town was changed to Athelstan."

I found one reference about Iona, stating, "Iona was on the Iowa State line, east of Athelstan. (Map of Mo., 1884.) It is no longer listed." If Iona was listed as a town on an 1884 map, it would have been in existence for at least three years before the railroad came to town.

An 1894 street map for Athelstan states "originally Iona City". More research is needed on this. And it's not really important to the story of these quilt squares. It's just an interesting sidebar for me because my mom's name is Iona, and to have a town with that name so closely connect to the town where these quilt squares originated from piques my interest.

To further my confusion about Athelstan, the original article also states that "At the time the railway was built there existed a 'gallon' store on the Missouri side, two drug stores ..." It sounds as if 1887 Athelstan already existed on both sides of the border.

While all reference I've found refers to Athelstan, Iowa, I've discovered two references for Athelstan, Missouri.

A genealogy for Miles Sherman Gillidett references Rebecca Halleck Gillidett Small (Dr. Frederick Small being her second husband). It says: "Mrs. Rebecca Small, who died at Athelstan, Missouri, March 22, 1889, and is buried there." Checking the cemetery list for Athelstan Cemetery, clearly located in Iowa, to the northeast portion of town, along the Platte River, shows that Rebecca Small is buried there.

An obituary for John Alvin Swett, on December 8, 1966, states "Those from out of town attending the last rites of John Alvin Swett were...Henry Young of Athelstan, Missouri." Regardless of the questions of when Athelstan began, and how much of the city was on each side of either Iowa or Missouri, Athelstan existed then, even if it didn't stand the test of time.

Early Athelstan Commerce

At one time Athelstan was a bustling little burg. Never as large as Bedford, the county seat about eighteen miles away, it still had its share of commerce. Besides the 'gallon' store on the Missouri side, the reprinted article mentions these businesses:

Charles Merrill, drugstore

Mr. Winston, drugstore

Ace Nighswonger, general store

Hal Brown, general store

Miles Martin (first postmaster), general store

W.J.W. & Pearl Townsend, store

Sid Merriman, store

Miles Martin (postmaster & general store owner), hotel

Ed and Avon Johnson, butchers and sausage makers

Flint and Coats, coopers

Dr. Childres, first physician

Schoenmann and Sons, lumber yard

According to Wikipedia, "Traditionally, a cooper is someone who makes wooden staved vessels of a conical form, of greater length than breadth, bound together with hoops and possessing flat ends or heads. Examples of a cooper's work include but are not limited to casks, barrels, buckets, tubs, butter churns, hogsheads, firkins, tierces, rundlets, puncheons, pipes, tuns, butts, pins, and breakers."

Miles Washington Martin was a prominent Athelstan resident. Leaving his new wife and his buried infant son, he joined the 9th Iowa Calvary and fought in the Civil War for three and a half years. Returning to Athelstan he became the first postmaster, in late 1887 or early 1888, after the railroad came through and Iona was formed. According to the information in the article on Athelstan history, he also had a general store and operated a hotel. When the Athelstan Baptist Church was organized in 1897, he transferred his membership from Mt. Zion Baptist Church. He lived in Athelstan until his death 3/10/1933, two days shy of his 92nd birthday, six weeks after his wife Nancy's death. Miles Martin was the last civil war veteran in Athelstan at the time of his death.

Martin, his wife Nancy, his infant son David and daughter Maud Barber (1866-1946) are all buried in Athelstan Cemetery.

This historical account mentions a lumber yard, operated by Schoenmann & Sons. Ferdinand Schoenmann (b. 1858, Wisconsin) married 'Carrie' Caroline Mary (b. 1859, Wisconsin) in 1878. They moved to Iowa in 1886, with their two boys, George and Lorenzo. On April 12, 1899, they moved to Athelstan and began operating a lumber yard. The family moved to Blockton on September 12, 1900, but continued business as the Athelstan lumber yard.

Ferdinand and Carrie were highly regarded in Athelstan. Ferdinand was renowned for truth and sobriety. He loved music and was a chorister of the Methodist Episcopal Church for many years.

He died in 1918, at the age of fifty-nine. Carrie died three years later, in 1921, at the age of sixty-two. Her obituary states that Carrie was at the lumber yard on the Saturday evening before her death, from 4 pm to 6 pm. She called on neighbors on the way home, appeared to be in good health and died that evening.

At that time the sons, George and Lorenzo, had been working at the lumber yard for several years. Lorenzo returned to farming near Blockton and then opened a hardware store in Blockton in 1922, so it appears that they sold the business following their mother's death.

Lake of Three Fires

The Pottawattomi tribe reportedly traveled the prairies of southwestern Iowa and northwestern Missouri. They were a large group of Native Americans and were known as the 'Fire Nation'. Local legend tells that two other tribes joined them, to form a confederacy known as 'Three Fires'. The story goes that the three tribes formed a council to join forces as protection against other invading tribes.

Runners were sent to wandering nations to tell of the rendezvous. Smoke from three fires signaled the exact location. The fires were built at the tops of the highest hills, so that smoke could be seen from any direction. The three fires were kept burning as long as the three tribes joined together. If any of the fires went out, it meant that the tribes had left the area to continue on their own.

One of these fire sites overlooked the valley that is now filled with the waters of Lake of Three Fires. When a state park was built in this area of Iowa and dedicated in 1935, it was named Lake of Three Fires State Park, in honor of the legend of the three fires.

In 1934, when these quilt squares were made, the new state park was merely a potential project. A state lake fund had been established and businesses and community members were contributing to the project. It hadn't been named Lake of Three Fires yet.

The Bedford Times-Press reported on March 14, 1935: 'Lake Lexington Park', or whatever the new state lake and park are to be called, will be developed and improved by federal funds, according to reports reaching here, and much of the work is to be done the coming spring and summer."

The article reports that the 384-acres will be entirely fenced by a seven-foot woven wire, topped with three strands of barbed wire. Inside the fenced area will be improved roads and paths, and shelter houses of limestone. Provisions were made for the culture and care of fish in the artificial lake.

The 900-foot dam, with concrete spillways, will use limestone slabs to protect it from weather and wave erosion.

"It is believed a CCC camp will be established in the vicinity, the boys assisting relief workers in the vast amount of work to be done at the lake and park during the coming months."

The newspaper was correct. CCC workers did assist in the construction of the dam and lake.

Leona (Byrns) Stevenson stated that her father, Vernie Byrns, was one of the CCC workers that helped build this local landmark. With jobs being scarce and men thankful for any jobs they could get, I'm fairly sure that many other local men helped build the dam and the lake also.

The lake is 93-acres in size, with three miles of shoreline. The deepest point is fourteen feet deep. Fishermen can catch an assortment of fish, including Bluegill, Channel Catfish, Flathead Catfish, Largemouth Bass and White Crappie.

1934

The year these quilt squares were made, 1934, was not an easy year. The nation was still reeling from the aftermath of the Great Depression. Banks had failed, including the one in Athelstan. Families lost their savings and their jobs. Farms were foreclosed on. Families did what they had to in order to survive.

If this wasn't enough to deal with, four years of drought, record-breaking heat and dust storms that plagued large portions of the country added to the troubles. Drought reduced the US corn crop. The average yield per acre fell to 15.7 bushels, down from 22.8 in 1933.

The government tried to step in and help the farmers. A Farm Mortgage Financing Act, passed by Congress January 31, created a Federal Farm Mortgage Corporation to help farmers whose mortgages were being foreclosed. A Crop Loan Act, passed February 23rd, authorized loans to farmers to tide them over until harvest time. And on June 28th, the Frazier-Lemke Farm Bankruptcy Act passed, allowing mortgage foreclosures to be postponed for five years.

Prices in 1934

Prices were much different in 1934. They had to be when the average wages were around $1,500 to $1,600 a year.

It still took a long time to save up enough for a new house, which averaged $5,900. Renting was cheaper in those days, averaging around $20 a month.

New cars cost around $575, while a new Studebaker truck was $625. Gas for the vehicles, depending which source you look at, reports that it cost from 10¢ to 19¢ per gallon. Food was much cheaper than today. As long as you don't compare it to the pittance people received in wages back then. A loaf of bread was 8¢. Hamburger meat costs 12¢ a pound. One source reports that milk was 45 cents a gallon and eggs were 53¢ a dozen.

A man's shirt costs a whole $2.50. That sounds so reasonable now, but if you figure that that was 12.5% of what you paid for rent, then it seems pretty steep. Rents here in our area right now run from $800 a month for the cheapest apartment to $1200 for a house. Using the same 12.5%, that would make a shirt in the area of $100 - $150 today, if we increased prices to match this percentage.

Postage stamps were $0.03 each. They had a long run at this price, from November 3, 1917, to July 31, 1958.

Bonnie & Clyde

The notorious Depression-area duo, Bonnie Parker and Clyde Barrow, along with other members of their gang spent the early 1930s on a crime spree, robbing small-town restaurants, banks, and gas stations, killing twelve people in the process. They were never in one place for long as they traveled throughout Texas, Oklahoma, Missouri, and Iowa, on the lookout for easy targets and quick get-aways. In 1933, Bonnie and Clyde, along with Clyde's brother Buck, Buck's wife Blanche, and their accomplice W.D. Jones, were nearly captured in Dexter, Iowa, about thirty-three miles west of Des Moines.

They arrived at Dexfield Park, an abandoned amusement park near Dexter, on July 19 or 20, 1933, following a gun battle with officers in Platte City, Missouri. Buck and his wife Blanche were injured. They camped out in the woods near Dexter, and Clyde went into town a few times to shop for food and clothing, buying chicken, pies, and soda pop. Since they couldn't go to the hospital for treatment, Clyde also bought gauze and tape to treat Buck's wound.

It's reported that on Sunday, July 23rd, a local farmer, Henry Nye, discovered their campsite by chance. He reported the bloody bandages, burning car mats, and the bullet-ridden car he had seen to John Love, Dexter night marshal, who in turn called Dallas County sheriff Clinton Knee in Adel. Knee, along with

71

about fifty other lawmen, including some from the Des Moines Police Department, surrounded the Barrow encampment. They were met with a barrage of gunfire from the gangsters, and after an extended gun battle, Clyde, Bonnie, and W.D. Jones escaped through an unguarded route over the South Raccoon River. Buck, too seriously wounded to go on, stayed behind, and Blanche stayed with him.

The escapees made their way to the nearby Vallie Feller farm, where they stole a car and fled. In Polk City, they abandoned the car, now bloodstained and with a shattered window, stole another car, and subsequently were reported seen in LuVerne, Sutherland, and Denison, Iowa, and even in Des Moines, although the sightings didn't yield any results.

Buck Barrow died in a Perry hospital five days after the incident. Blanche Barrow was returned to Missouri and sentenced to ten years in prison for her part.

By 1934, Bonnie and Clyde were back in Iowa. They robbed the First State Bank at Rembrandt, the State Savings Bank in Knierim, and were suspected of robbing other banks in Stuart and Lamoni.

They were on the run for several months, until May 23, 1934, when the pair's journey of crime came to an end in a hail of bullets fifty miles east of Shreveport, Louisiana. The father of one of the gang members informed police where to watch for them. Texas Ranger Frank Hamer, sheriff's deputy Ted C. Hinton, and four other sheriff's deputies set up an ambush on the road. Bonnie and Clyde drove into the trap and were riddled with bullets, ending their four statewide crime spree. Clyde died holding a Thompson submachine gun and Bonnie died with a sawed-off shotgun in her hands.

The Dust Bowl

The heat and drought of several years, in the aftermath of imprudent plowing during the Great War, when farmers planted virgin lands in wheat to cash in on high grain prices, set in motion the phenomenon known as 'The Dust Bowl', which peaked in 1934. This was the worst year of drought in US history, covering more than 75% of the country and severely affecting twenty-seven of our forty-eight states.

Four heat shattering records were set in Iowa in 1934. In May, Inwood reached 111 degrees. In June, Lamoni met that record, hitting 111 degrees also. Keokuk, Iowa topped those highs, hitting 118 degrees in July and 116 degrees in August.

The worst dust storm of the year began May 9th, in Montana and Wyoming. Severe winds lifted an estimated 350-million tons of brown earth skyward, where they were swept eastward across the Dakotas. By late afternoon, the storm front moved east and reached Dubuque, Iowa and Madison, Wisconsin and headed towards Chicago, filling every surface along the way with dust and dirt.

By that evening, the monstrous dust storm began depositing 12-million pounds of dust on Chicago – four pounds of dust for each resident of the city.

By midday, May 10th, the storm reached Buffalo, New York and kept going. Moving at close to 100 mph, by the next morning, it was spreading its deposit on Boston, New York, Washington, and Atlanta before heading out to the Atlantic Ocean, where it dusted ships that were sitting three hundred miles offshore.

The *United Press* reported that the dust cloud was as much as 1,500 miles long, 900 miles across and two miles high. It has smothered nearly one-third of our nation. Approximately 35-million acres of land were essentially destroyed for crop production and 100-million acres had lost all or most of their topsoil.

Fireside Chats by FDR

The President, Franklin Delano Roosevelt (FDR), held a series of six nationwide speeches, called Fireside Chats, four in 1933 and two in 1934. Most of the nation sat entranced around radios, listening to what the President had to say.

Sunday, March 12, 1933: On the Bank Crisis.

Sunday, May 7, 1933: Outlining the New Deal Program.

Monday, July 24, 1933: On the Purposes and Foundations of the Recovery Program.

Sunday, October 22, 1933: On the Currency Situation

Thursday, June 28, 1934: Review of the Achievements of the Seventy-third Congress.

Sunday, September 30, 1934: On Moving Forward to Greater Freedom and Greater Security.

Milestones 1932 – 1934:

Here are some milestones for 1932-1934, leading up to the days when these quilt blocks were lovingly embroidered by community members in Athelstan, Iowa.

1932   First plastic coated paper milk cartons introduced commercially.

1932   Use of carbon dioxide tested as a method to retard produce decay; eventually led to a method for protecting fruits in transit.

1932   The Revenue Act creates the first gasoline tax in the U.S. (1 cent per gallon).

The Mars Bar, candy bar, was introduced.

Prohibition (the 18th amendment) is repealed.

1933   Proctor & Gamble began marketing 'Dreft,' the first synthetic detergent for home use. Detergents perform better in hard water than soaps.

1933   The first great dust storm occurred on the Great Plains.

1933   Kit Kat candy bar invented.

1933   A California packer was able to homogenize peanuts into a stable butter - 'Skippy Churned Peanut Butter'.

1933   Kraft Miracle Whip Salad Dressing is introduced by National Dairy Products. It combines the best features of two existing products -- mayonnaise and boiled salad dressing. It soon grows to outsell mayonnaise in the U.S.A.

1933   Soil Erosion Service established, later known as Soil Conservation Service, and today as Natural Resources Conservation Service.

The first farm bill, the Agricultural Adjustment Act was passed by Congress to maintain a balance between production and consumption of agricultural commodities.

The worst drought in U.S. history took place in the Great Plains and covered over 75 percent of the country.

1934   Taylor Grazing Act gave U.S. Department of the Interior power to regulate grazing on public lands in the West.

1934   May - One of the worst dust storms ever to hit the Great Plains occurred. It lasted two days and the area lost massive amounts of topsoil.

1934   Pepsi introduced their 12-ounce bottle for the same price competitors were selling 6-ounce bottles.

1934   Donald Duck's first appearance.

1934   Ritz Crackers were introduced by the National Biscuit Company (now Nabisco).

Shirley Temple in 1934

Shirley Temple was signed with Education, until it declared bankruptcy in September 1933. In February 1934, she signed a contract with Fox Films. She started with bit parts and was loaned out to Paramount and Warner Bros.-First National.

In April 1934, *Stand Up and Cheer!* became her breakthrough film. She received widespread critical acclaim and truckloads of fan mail. Her salary was raised to $1,250 a week. In June 1934, her popularity rose with a follow-up film, *Little Miss Marker*.

She finished 1934 with the December 28th release of *Bright Eyes*—the first feature film crafted specifically for her and the first in which her name was above the title. In the film's one musical number, she introduced what would become her signature song, *On the Good Ship Lollipop*. The song was an instant hit and sold 500,000 sheet music copies.

Her films were seen as generating hope and optimism, and President Franklin D. Roosevelt said, "It is a splendid thing that for just a fifteen cents an American can go to a movie and look at the smiling face of a baby and forget his troubles."

Her fame didn't stop with movies. In 1934, Benjamin Michtom, president of the Ideal Toy and Novelty Co., obtained the exclusive rights to the Shirley Temple doll. Renowned doll artist Bernard Lipfert was asked to design the mold.

In the October 1934 issue of *Playthings* magazine, Ideal announced that it would produce an exact replica of Shirley Temple, in doll form, in time for Christmas.

Shirley Temple's popularity did not escape Iowa.

That year, *The Bedford Times-Press* held a 'Kid Party', a free picture show for the community children. These annual shows were sponsored by local merchants and had huge turnouts.

The merchants listed, where parents could get the free tickets from included: Rankin Shoe Store, Oak Barber Shop, Rhoad's Drug Store, Iowa-Nebraska Light & Power Co., Opera House Café, Robinson Produce, Dr. John F. Hardin, Weingarth Shoe Repair, Paul's Pantorium, The New Grill, Ahrens Drug Store, Paschal Clo. Co., Dr. G. W. Rimel, Taylor Used Furniture Store, Harbour & Son Produce, Hawkeye Lumber Co., Charles Wieser's Garage, Frank Beebe Garage, Atty. James R. Locke, Dr. J.S. Terrill, O,K. Coffee Shop, Swift Produce Co., The Style Shoppe, Atty James A. Lucas, B. Prugh & Sons, Wisdom & Kirketeg, Dr. M. R. Francis, H.C. Little, Dr. C. W. Steward, Mary-Alice Shop, Dr. K.B. Paschal, Gamble Store Agency, I. W. Bristow, Kolterman's Store, Bedford Candy Kitchen, Pote Drug Store, Thompson Merc. Co., Morris Market and Grocery, Bedford Times-Press, Bray Motor Co., Pik 'N Pay, Rialto Theatre, FullerTaylor Clo. Co., Worley-Severs & Co., J. M. Little, Ray Johnson, and Dr. J.T. Maloy.

From *Bedford Times-Press*

(Image used with permission)

Depression-Era Quilting

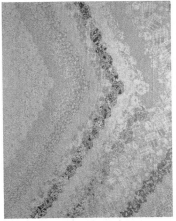

A variation of a 'Diamond Field' quilt, displayed at Farmer's Dotter.

World's Fair Century of Progress: In 1933, this quiltmaking competition at the Chicago World's Fair offered a grand prize of $1,000, plus $25 for regional winters. This generated interest in quilting, as times were lean and this chance to make money was welcomed.

Weekly Newspaper Columns: Newspapers carried regular columns with quilting patterns. The *Kansas City Star* began printing quilt patterns in 1926. In May 1933, the popular *'Nancy Page Quilt Club'*, by Florence LaGanke Harris, began a regular Tuesday Quilt Club, which featured pieced and appliquéd patterns to complete an entire quilt. Another popular quilt designer, Ruby Short McKim, was a regular newspaper feature through the 1920's and 1930's. At one time her syndicated column appeared in over 900 U.S. newspapers.

Fabrics: The wisdom of the time was "Use up, wear out, make do, or do without." A scrap bag was common in most households. Salvageable pieces of worn out clothing were used for scraps to mend other clothes or piece into quilts. The fabric sacking used for feed, flour, sugar, seed, meal and salt bags began to be printed fabrics. This fabric was used for clothing, dish towels, diapers, nightgowns, underwear (very scratchy according to my mother, to her dismay) and quilt pieces. Three feed sacks were needed to make a woman's dress. Novelty sacks were often printed for dolls or aprons.

Colors: The pastels of the 1920's began to get brighter and more intense. Dye colors began to get more reliable with newer methods. The number of colors used in prints began to increase. Contrasting color combinations were used more frequently.

- Nile Green or Mint Green was popular, especially in combination with Rose Pink (presently referred to as Bubble Gum Pink).

- Pastel blues were not as popular, being replaced by medium and darker blues.

- Yellows became more golden, especially in combination with brown, along with Lemon & Canary Yellow.

- Lilacs and lavenders were popular

- Red/Black/White combinations were popular

- Red was a clear, bright, chemical red or an imitation of the Turkey Red of the 1800's.

- Burgundy as a deep-colored print made a comeback in the late 1930's.

Prints: Prints became busier with more colors added. Bright colors in contrasting combinations were popular. Prints became larger in scale than the prints of the 1920's. Black accents began to be used as a design feature in the 1930's.

Quilting Patterns: The most popular patterns from this period are: Double Wedding Ring, Dresden Plate, Grandmother's Flower Garden, Fans, Sunbonnet Sues, Yo-Yo's and Redwork. Embroidery made a come-back. Appliqué with black buttonhole stitching around each piece was distinctive.

Rooms at Farmer's Dotter quilting retreat, along with a garden shot from outside

The Birth of
Sunbonnet Sue's

While Sunbonnet Sue's were one of the most popular quilting patterns in the 1930's, along with Dresden Plate, Grandmother's Flower Garden and Double Wedding Ring, her origins didn't begin there. Her journey had started thirty or forty years earlier.

KATE GREENAWAY

British artist Kate Greenaway, a children's book, and fashion illustrator was a huge factor in the development of the well-known Sunbonnet Sue pattern. Her work was widely published in the 1880's and 1890's. In America, her artistry was featured in Ladies Home Journal and Harper's.

While not exactly the images of the Sunbonnet Sue that we typically see or imagine, her drawings of bonneted children was most likely the inspiration that led to the creation of our own bonneted beloved American.

Greenaway's innocent children are in peaceful, serene English country settings, never in scenes that include cities, trains, or factories. They're seeming without any cares, playful and cavorting, portraying a youthful innocence.

BERTHA CORBETT

"We must help pick the apples."

An American illustrator, Bertha Corbett, was an active artist at the turn of the century. Her work was influenced by the popular Greenaway's illustrations, although Corbett – as with most artists – used the inspiration and put her own stamp and imagery to create her own unique artwork.

Eulalie Osgood, a New Hampshire schoolteacher, was writing a children's primer. Around 1895, she contacted Corbett about illustrating her book. The joint collaboration was successful and Sunbonnet Babies Primer was born.

Corbett clothed her children in out of date fashions and placed them in predominately rural settings. While a few boy figures found their way into the Primer, most drawings were of bonneted little girls participating in a variety of activities. Large sunbonnets completely covered the girl's faces, no facial features showing on any of the children.

The Sunbonnet Babies Primer was wildly successful. By 1910, over 1.3 million copies were sold.

The Sunbonnet babies were reproduced in many graphics products. They appeared on postcards, wallpaper, wrapping paper and even on china dishes.

BERNHARDT WALL

Other sunbonnet girls began appearing. Another American artist created a popular line of sunbonnet girls around the same time.

Bernhardt Wall, an accomplished artist, opened a studio in 1894. He closed it when he enlisted in the Spanish-American War. When he returned, a picture frame company - Ullman Manufacturing Company, - contracted him for pictures to help sell their frames. The company moved into the burgeoning postcard business, and Wall illustrated  many postcards for them. His first series featured a little girl in a red dress, wearing a large white bonnet. Her face also was hidden from view. Wall's bonneted girl appeared in activities related to the days of the week. Monday was wash day, Tuesday was for ironing – all the way through the week until Saturday's baking day. Later that year he produced a Months of the Year series. The postcards were immensely popular and soon Wall was represented by no fewer than fifteen postcard companies.

In 1907, under the pen name Uncle Milton, he wrote a book featuring his designs – Little Susie Sunbonnet and How Her Year Was Spent, A Story for Little Tots.

EMBROIDERY BEFORE QUILTING

The first printed embroidery pattern for a bonneted little girl was in the February 1888 issue of Harper's. Initially, these embroidered, outlined designs were very popular, most often appearing on dish towels and flour sack towels.

Sunbonnet Sue quilt applique patterns were issued around 1900 by Ladies Art Patterns, but they weren't included in their catalogs until after 1923. The patterns were available either as a stamped design on cloth or as cutout patterns for applique. McCall's Pattern Company also issued a similar version, which was available from about 1900 through the 1930's.3999

NEWSPAPER PATTERNS TO HISTORY

Although the embroidery and quilting patterns had been available for many years, when newspapers began printing weekly quilting patterns in the 1920's and 1930's, the popularity seemed to skyrocket. The easier availability of the patterns, coupled with the post-depression years as women had to make do with what they could, created an atmosphere where hand-sewn quilts and handwork would flourish.

Many years later, most anyone associated with quilting or handwork in any manner will know what you mean when you mention any of the well-known names - Sunbonnet Sue, Bonnie Bonnet, Sun Bonnet Baby, Dutch Doll, Overall Sam or Overall Bill. Whether the little girls are working, playing, getting into trouble, or simply standing there are many are, they're well loved by many. (And sometimes not. Believe it or not, not everyone adores these patterns from the past. But that's another chapter.)

There is an obvious shift in the overall design, as the earlier sunbonnet girls from the turn of the century are distinctly different from those created in the 1930's. However, even upon viewing only a few different designs, it's immediately apparent that there's not only one design.

Even amongst the thirty squares in this one set, there are vast differences from one square to another. The ladies and young girls from this small town, from the same quilting guild, didn't use the same exact pattern. There are differences in the bonnet size and shape, the shape of the hands and feet, even the dresses differ. Stitching applications varied from one to another. It's apparent from square to square on who had more stitchery experience and finesse. And the extra little touches are different on each. Some, like the three unsigned squares, merely were appliqued to the muslin backing with neat and functional stitches. Others added more decorative stitches, such as Eva Byrnes or Katie Kemery, who embellished their hats with ornamental hat bands and brims. And then there was Jean Marie Carroll, who modified her sunbonnet to something more reminiscent of a 1920's flapper hat.

These women may have had a hard life, providing for their families and making do with very little in this tiny little farm town without a lot of money. But they loved and cared for their families. They loved and cared for their neighbors. And they found little bits of pleasure and creativity wherever they could, modifying the history of the Sunbonnet Sues to make their own distinctive piece of history.

The End of Athelstan

The population on the 1925 census shows 146 names. When the previously mentioned undated *Bedford Times-Press* article was written (my estimate is around 1941, from the previous mention of JW Large's son's death) it says:

"Athelstan, although diminished in population from earlier years, now has an accredited school and a population of 141."

From there, the population dwindled to thirty-one people by 1990. By the 2000 census, the population fell to eighteen residents and in 2004, the city was dis-incorporated.

Athelstan may no longer exist as a functioning, thriving city, however, its memories remain, alive forever, in the hearts of the descendants of those who lived in this outlying area of Iowa, balancing on the uppermost Missouri border. Time may pass, but some things remain, beloved memories of a time long past – difficult days, yet fondly remembered by those still here.

Formerly the old bank. After the bank failed, the Post Office was here. The store that wrapped around the corner post office was Verna Jenkin's market.

The middle of the street, about where I'm standing to take the picture above, is where the east/west Iowa/Missouri state line runs. From my visit to Athelstan, I could truly see how the town grew up on both sides of the border, existing in both states at one time. I enjoyed my time spent there that August afternoon. On one side of the street, I was in Iowa. We stepped across the street to chat with a remaining resident. Whoopie! Now I was in Missouri. Oops, there we go, a few steps away and now I'm back in Iowa.

The view from outside the cemetery, as it overlooks what
remains of Athelstan.

The Quilt Squares Come Home

In 2014 I delivered the quilt squares to the Taylor County Historical Museum, just a few miles from their birthplace in Athelstan, Iowa. These squares that were lovingly stitched by hand went from Iowa to California during their almost seventy years with Doris. In the next ten years, they followed me from California, to Arizona, and to Texas before I packed them up and took them on an airplane back home to Iowa.

The day before the Quilt Tea at the museum, I had the most memorable afternoon. I met Rosalyn, Leona, and Bonnie for a delicious lunch in Bedford and an afternoon tour of Athelstan and the cemetery, followed by a great fish dinner at the café.

Lt to Rt: Leona Stephenson, Pat Nance, Rosalyn Cummings, Bonnie Polston

The day of the Quilt Tea dawned bright and sunny. Over seventy people came to see the quilt squares returned home. Memories were shared. Several women brought pictures from early Athelstan and of the loved ones represented by these squares.

Ellen Lemke, then a spritely 99 year-young woman, read a poem of hers and shared her thoughts about quilting and how it relates to life. I am honored that I had a chance to meet Ellen, who continued volunteering at the museum until shortly before her passing at the age of 102.

My favorite part of the weekend – and there were so many delightful memories made – was meeting descendants and loved ones of the women and men represented on these quilt squares from the past. The memories of loved ones past that are stitched in time on these thirty pieces of muslin is remembered by the legacy they've left in their descendants.

The day would not have been the success that it was without the tireless hard work of the many dedicated museum volunteers. They cleaned. They set up tables and chairs. They hosted. They served. They kept bringing out chairs when the people kept flowing through the doors. They were hospitable and treated everyone as honored guests.

I've been associated with many museums and organizations throughout the years and I have to commend these special Iowa residents. I have never seen such a great volunteer team. They have the biggest hearts and share a love of honoring the Iowa history they are caretakers of. They are the greatest and deserve recognition for dedication and contributions of their time and energy.

Sunbonnet Sue cake by Bonnie Polston

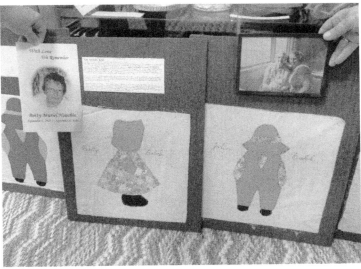

Squares for Betty and John Balch, pictured with Betty's memorial and a photograph of Betty with her mother, Grace Hayes. Taken at the museum's Quilt Tea.

Keeping Athelstan Alive

**"...people die twice: when they physically die,
and when we stop telling stories about them.**

-- Carol LaChapelle, *Finding Your Voice, Telling Your Stories*

**"There are three deaths. The first is when the body ceases to function.
The second is when the body is consigned to the grave.
The third is that moment, sometime in the future, when your name is
spoken for the last time."**

-- David Eagleman, *Sum: Forty Tales from the Afterlives*

**"Someday soon, perhaps in forty years, there will be no one alive who has
ever known me. That's when I will be truly dead - when I exist in no one's
memory. I thought a lot about how someone very old is the last living
individual to have known some person or cluster of people.
When that person dies, the whole cluster dies, too, vanishes from the
living memory. I wonder who that person will be for me.
Whose death will make me truly dead?"**

-- Irvin D. Yalom, *Love's Executioner and Other Tales of Psychotherapy*

To honor the women and young girls that embellished these
pieces of muslin over eighty years ago, here are a few of the
granite monuments marking their earthly resting place.

Knowing that so many are buried in Athelstan Cemetery, I was
drawn to visit the cemetery as a pay tribute to their memories.
Rosalyn, Bonnie, and Leona graciously spent the day with me on
my Iowa visit, stepping back in time as we traveled the roads of
Athelstan and stopped at the cemetery to pay our respects. What
fun we had, driving the dusty, dirt roads as the memories flew.
We truly kept many memories alive that day.

To avoid the third death, the day that someone's name is spoken for the last time, here are a few of the gravestones of people commemorated on the Athelstan quilt squares. More people and family members are buried here than these few, but to include them all would be another whole book.

Nellie and Charles Morris, Doris Morris' parents

Evelyn Bownes

Maxine Bownes

Georgia Older

Mrs. E.J. Bownes (Eliza Jane, Georgia Older's mother)

Eva Byrns, 18-month old Leona Byrns mother

John Balch, brother to Betty Balch

Bedford, Iowa, Taylor County

The first courthouse for Taylor County was begun in 1863. It was constructed of stone on the south side of the square. Additional office space was rented as the county grew and required more space for county government.

The cornerstone for the present courthouse was laid in June 1892. The three-story Romanesque Revival building was completed in the spring the following year. It was constructed of pressed brick and Bedford stone. A large dome tops the building. The interior features fireplaces in most of the rooms. The building was built for $38,000. Because the contractor lost money on the project the county gave him an additional $1,000 and a gold watch for adhering to the original contract price.

Years of history reside in the vintage vaults in the courthouse.

The courthouse has many still functional architectural features.
The fireplaces, while still functional, have been sealed off to keep the bats
from entering the courthouse.

Taylor County Historical Museum

The Taylor County Historical Museum is a treasure trove of goodies. There are many other quilts exhibited there, besides these quilt squares. Be aware, with so many vintage items to share, the displays are often rotated to showcase new items.

Besides an abundance of historical quilts and memorabilia, the museum complex also includes a round barn, 110-year-old log cabin, furnished rural schoolhouse, restored caboose and old depot, museum building, print shop, bank building and a small chapel.

114

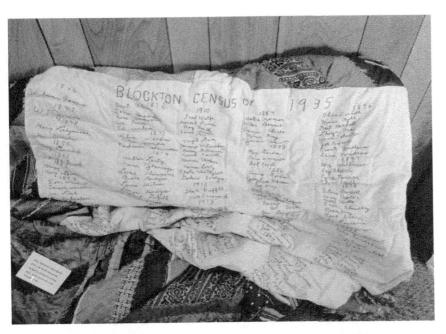

Quilt made by Celestia Seymour Smith, between 1834 & 1917. Given by the Laverne Irwin Estate.

Name Quilt made 1930 by Oak Hill
Ladies Aid. Purchased by Zona Posten.
Given by Bernadine Bender
Oak Hill Bible Class of 1930. Sold at
auction by the church to Zona Posten.

Friendship quilt made about 1905 as a
money making project for the Siam
Christian Church. Given by Frank and
Fannie Shields.

Another museum jewel is the J.E. Cameron round barn, built south of Lenox, in 1907. The deteriorated barn was split into two sections and moved to its present site at the museum and renovated, using original materials wherever possible. The barn is 50 feet high, 70 feet in diameter and 220 feet in circumference. A circular track hangs from the haymow floor supporting a Louden Litter Bucket.

The Judson Beemer house. The Beemer's (Judson, wife Esther, and three sons) moved to Iowa in a covered wagon in 1878.

Count your blessings –
Stitch them one by one.
~Author Unknown

> I apologize for the black and white photos included in this book. They don't really do the squares justice, yet the cost of printing in color is so high that to produce the same exact book, with color pictures, would double the price of the book.
>
> I'd like for you to be able to see the quilt squares in full color. If you've purchased this book and would like to see the color photos, please email me at texastrishafaye@yahoo.com. Put **FREE QUILT SQUARE PDF** in the subject line and **send a copy of your receipt**. I'll email you a digital copy of this book.

Thank you for reading *Memories on Muslin*, about the memories stitched in time on these quilt squares lovingly made in Athelstan, Iowa so many years ago. If you enjoyed it, won't you please take a moment to leave me a review at your favorite retailer?

Check out some of my other books about people and places long gone in *Fat and Sassy*, *Dear Arlie*, or in my collection of Vintage Daze short stories.

Have a blessed day!

Trisha

About the Author:

When not gardening or rescuing abandoned feral kittens, Trisha spends her days researching people, places, and pieces from the past. These connections are important to her and she likes to share these snippets with other people that have a love for people and days long gone.

Connect with me:

Visit my website trishafaye.com

Friend me on Facebook: facebook.com/trisha.faye.5

Follow me on Twitter: twitter.com/texastrishafaye

Discover other titles by Trisha Faye:
Fat and Sassy
Memory Gardens
Scooter's Tale: A Rescue Cat's Story
Trail Angel Mama
Wash on Monday
In Celebration of Mothers
In Celebration of Sisters

Vintage Daze Short Stories (ebooks only)
Dear Arlie: Postcards to a Friend (1907 – 1913)
Spinning a New Life in Texas
Hazel's Spice of Life
Fargo Women Plot and Plan

Coming soon:
Embracing 60
A Spoonful of Sugar

Made in the USA
Coppell, TX
11 April 2021